JAMIE SHULTZ

Intuitive Eating for Kids

Non-diet Healthy Food Options for Happy Tummies

Contents

Introduction

Parenting is a full-time job, and there are no breaks from it. One of the things all parents tend to worry about is diet and nutrition. Dieting is never recommended for children, but eating healthy is essential. So, what do you do? Are you trying to get your child to eat healthy but aren't sure where to begin? Well, intuitive eating is a brilliant protocol that can simplify your life.

There is a lot of confusion about intuitive eating and whether it is a safe and healthy option for kids. Even if parents want to start following the concept of intuitive eating, they are often unsure where to begin. Some might also be worried about their child indulging in unhealthy foods because intuitive eating doesn't discriminate between different types of foods. Even if they want to raise their children as intuitive eaters, they probably hesitate because they are unaware of any healthier food alternatives.

It is not just young kids, but even teens can start following the concept of intuitive eating. In fact, intuitive eating is for everyone.

Well, if you had similar doubts on your mind, then you don't have to worry much because this book will work as the perfect guide to intuitive eating. This book will help you understand what intuitive eating is and help you get started with its protocols. Intuitive eating is a simple way of eating which doesn't have anything to do with meal plans, diet, discipline, or even willpower. Instead, it teaches you to finally understand your body's cues of fullness, satisfaction, and hunger. It encourages you to trust your body and your ability to understand what it needs.

In this book, you will learn what intuitive eating means, the benefits it offers to your child, myths about intuitive eating, challenges you will need to overcome, and how you can teach your child to get started with intuitive eating. Apart from this, you will also learn about several healthier food alternatives that you can offer your child.

Children, as well as adults, tend to enjoy junk food. Instead of worrying about eating junk food, it is time to think of healthier alternatives for the same. You will find several healthier alternatives for the junk food your child probably loves. Within this book, you will find simple tips and advice you can start following to get your child to eat healthily.

You will not only be teaching your child about intuitive eating but will also be encouraging him to pick up healthy alternatives instead of junk food voluntarily. Well, this book is the guide you have been looking for. Once you are armed with all the advice and knowledge given in this book, you can start practicing intuitive eating while encouraging your child to do the same!

If you are ready to learn more about all this, then let us get started immediately.

1

Intuitive Eating 101

What is Intuitive Eating?

The concept of intuitive eating was created by two registered dieticians named Elyse Resch and Evelyn Tribole in 1995. Unlike various fad diets, intuitive eating assumes a non-diet pattern for improving health and wellness. It enables you to understand your body signals and break free of the cycle of chronic dieting while strengthening and healing your relationship with food. From the perspective of nutrition, intuitive eating provides a framework that ensures the interventions for proper nutrition based on behavior instead of restrictive practices and rules. It mainly helps you understand your body's signals of hunger, fullness, and satisfaction. Instead of providing a set of restrictive rules, it encourages you to get in touch with your body's internal cues.

We are all intuitive eaters, at least at birth. For instance, babies tend to cry whenever they are hungry and stop crying when they get food to eat. Likewise, even children tend to balance out their food intake. There will be days when they eat a lot and days when they don't eat much. Children know when they are hungry and how much food they need to eat. So, if we are all intuitive eaters, why do we have to learn about it again?

Well, as we start growing, the relationship we share with food also changes. We learn to manage our hunger and control our appetites. We all try to somehow live up to the societal notions of the perfect body shape. It is perhaps one of the main reasons why dieting is quite common in today's world. From trying to get washboard abs to a size zero figure, there are various notions associated with the idea of physical perfection. In our bid to try and get the ideal body shape, we all forget to concentrate on what our bodies need. The sad part is kids get influenced by this at a much younger age and fall in this vicious trap of beauty standards.

As we start growing older, there are different rules and restrictions we start following. We tend to lose touch with our inner intuitive eater. Most adults take pride in the fact that they finish everything that is served on their plate. Regardless of whether they want to eat or not, people hate wasting food. Well, it is a good idea to try and eliminate waste, but does your body need that extra serving of pasta? We also learn that a sweet treat can be a reward, or it can also be taken away when misbehaved. We are all regularly told that certain foods are bad, whereas certain foods are extremely good. For instance, during the '80s, fats were increasingly demonized, and a variety of low-fat and non-fat products started cropping up on the markets. During the early 2000s, we were told that fats are good for the body, and it is carbs that people need to avoid. The notion of good and bad foods kept changing as the research about food increased. Since we have all become adept at labeling foods as being either good or bad, there is some stigma and guilt associated with these so-called bad foods.

If you are following a diet, you might feel a little guilty if you binge on a pint of ice cream and forego the diet. We all experience this guilt whenever we eat these so-called unhealthy foods, and this kickstarts a negative relationship with food.

Unlike all the other diets available, intuitive eating is not a diet. It is a concept of eating. You don't have to count calories, track your macros, or even limit certain foods. There are no rules to follow. You can finally stop worrying about coming up with elaborate meal plans or measuring the portions you consume. In fact, all these things are discouraged in intuitive eating. Intuitive eating is all about relearning to step outside the diet mentality we have acquired. It is about trying to understand your internal cues of hunger, satisfaction, and fullness. Once you start trusting these internal cues or your intuition and move away from any external signals like restrictions or rules, you will be able to eat better and healthier automatically.

Once you start eating intuitively, you can finally eat whatever you want without experiencing any guilt. When you learn to trust your body, you will know what it needs. Once you start catering to your body's needs, your overall health and efficiency will increase. When you know what to eat, when to eat and how much you want to eat, you don't need any other regulations or rules. Your own body will regulate the eating habits you display, and there is plenty of freedom here. While following this simple idea, you don't have to worry about giving up your freedom. It is perhaps the main reason why intuitive eating is sustainable in the long run. Intuitive eaters know when they need to eat vegetables, and when they can have some dessert. You can do these things without feeling guilty about your choices.

Benefits of Intuitive Eating for Kids

Unlike traditional dieting, intuitive eating is never measured by weight loss. It is an ongoing journey that provides full freedom while establishing a better relationship with food. Intuitive eating has several physical, emotional, and mental benefits. So, by teaching your child to be an intuitive eater, you can improve his overall well-being.

One of the most apparent benefits of intuitive eating is the ability to detect and understand hunger cues. Usually, children know when they are hungry. Your child can quickly identify his hunger levels once he starts listening to his hunger cues. Instead of worrying about mealtimes, try to encourage your child to tell you when he's hungry. If he eats when he's hungry, the number of unhealthy snacks in between meals will reduce.

Since he can now differentiate between actual hunger and unnecessary cravings, he can regulate his appetite. If your child is cranky around dinner time, it is most likely caused by hunger. However, if he is cranky after eating, then the issue might be something else entirely. With intuitive eating, you are equipping him with different tools he needs to handle his emotions.

Intuitive eating prohibits using food as a coping mechanism. Once you stop making your kid feel better by giving his favorite snack, he can start talking about any problems he is experiencing. It makes him more aware of what he is feeling. Therefore, intuitive eating reduces unhealthy food dependencies.

Children will become adept at understanding the foods they like and don't like. Since external cues no longer dictate his hunger, he is free to explore different types of foods. His willingness to try different foods will increase. He might even realize that he never really liked the snacks he used to crave.

4

When you don't restrict any food items, your child's relation-ship with food will improve. Allow him to eat as much as he wants. For instance, when you give him half a cookie and tell him that's all he will get, he will start craving more. It is an underlying human tendency to crave things that are restricted. When he knows there are no restrictions, his desire to binge on foods will be reduced.

A leading cause of food disorders is an unhealthy relationship with food. The best way to prevent this problem from cropping up is by teaching your child to maintain a healthy relationship with food. As a society, we are all to be blamed for the unhealthy relationship most of us have with food. When foods are labeled as good or bad, there is an inherent stigma associated with them. Once you remove all these labels, the guilt associated with eating so-called "bad" foods will decrease.

Instead of forcing your child to eat something, encourage him to try different foods. Even a picky eater will be more open to trying new foods. The key is to be persistent. Learn to respect your child's wishes and don't force him. Apart from this, intuitive eating also ensures that your child gets all the nourishment he needs.

Do you often tell your kid to eat the last bite or that he is not supposed to waste food? He might listen to you at times. At times, he might end up hiding his food in the napkin, throwing it in the garbage bin when you aren't looking, or even feed it to the family pet! These types of actions or words tend to teach children to ignore their natural hunger cues. With intuitive eating, he will get a better idea of what he needs and how much he needs to eat.

Improved digestion is another benefit of intuitive eating. When your child gets all the nourishment his body needs, its ability to function optimally will increase. It, in turn, will elevate his energy levels. How do you feel when you stuff yourself with sodas and burgers? You tend to feel lazy and lethargic. Your energy levels are influenced by the food you consume. So, if your child eats unhealthy foods, even he will experience a drop in his energy levels. Once he starts noticing that he feels better after eating certain foods, he will want to eat healthier!

Intuitive eating is often related to positive physical as well as psychological outcomes. It is especially true when children are given the freedom to understand and honor their body's cues, without their parents trying to control it. When your child is aware of physical sensations of hunger and satiety but gets messages from adults that he possibly cannot be hungry or he needs to eat everything on the plate, it takes away his sense of autonomy. You can undoubtedly encourage, trick, or bribe your child to eat better, but it creates a negative relationship with food. Apart from this, it can also turn your child into a picky eater while increasing the occurrences of power struggles at the dinner table. With intuitive eating, all these problems can be easily fixed.

2

The Do's And Don'ts Of Intuitive Eating

Obstacles To Intuitive Eating

There are plenty of benefits of intuitive eating. Raising your child as an intuitive eater will be quite helpful to him in the long run. However, making a change is never easy, even if it is essential for growth. In this section, let us look at certain obstacles parents usually run into when it comes to introducing intuitive eating to their kids.

Challenge #1: Children don't listen

Regardless of how much you wish your child would eat healthier food, he will not always listen to you. Kids don't necessarily eat the kind of food their parents want them to. It is one of the most common challenges a lot of parents come across. Usually, children tend to be a little rigid while dealing with changes. They can also be picky and slow. So, don't be surprised if your child isn't readily on board with the idea of making all sorts of healthier changes to his regular diet. It becomes a little more challenging, especially when parents start telling their children what and how much they are supposed to eat. Everyone likes challenging authority, and the same applies to your child as well. Instead of forcing things on him, try easing him into this process. Start by introducing one healthier alternative every day and wait for him to warm up to the idea that healthy food is tasty too.

Once you stop interfering with the way your child eats, you will finally be able to understand the kind of food your child likes and dislikes. All this information certainly comes in handy when you start looking for different ways to present new foods to your child. Intuitive eating is more about guiding your child instead of trying to control him.

Challenge #2: Food isn't a parenting tool

It is quite difficult to resist the urge to use food as a parenting tool. Regardless of what the situation is, never use food for parenting your child. Encouraging your child's good behavior by promising him his favorite meal or taking it away from him when he misbehaves are bad ideas. By doing this, your child forms unhealthy associations with food. For instance, he might start worrying that his favorite food will no longer be available to him if he doesn't clean his room. A child shouldn't have to worry about these things. No food is ever off-limits. Once you follow this rule, you will realize that your child is more willing to experiment with the different foods you offer.

Apart from this, your child might do something or behave like you would want him to only because he knows he will be rewarded. So, once the rewards stop, good behavior will stop too.

Challenge #3: Quantity of food

If your child is smaller or larger than an average child, then it can be a little difficult to accept how much he eats. To be honest, the quantity of food a child consumes is difficult for a parent to accept. Usually, parents, in their bid to prevent their child from feeling hungry soon after mealtime, stuff them with plenty of food. Apart from this, parents also have issues accepting the amount of certain foods their child eats. Your child might love eating sweets all the time or maybe he refuses to eat food if it isn't spaghetti. Well, all parents have to deal with these things.

Your child will learn to regulate his food intake once he has the autonomy to decide when and how much he eats. Apart from this, it also removes any pressure associated with eating while making him feel more comfortable with his body. If you are worried about the quantity of food your child eats, talk to your pediatrician about it. Some children tend to fill up rather easily, while others have a large appetite.

Challenge #4: Not the same as you

You might love your child to bits, but remember that your child is a separate entity from you. Never associate your internal cues of hunger with that of your child. Even if you feel hungry at seven in the evening, it doesn't mean your child needs to have dinner at that time. Learn to differentiate between these two things. Also, give your child a little freedom. Instead of lecturing him to make healthier choices, start showcasing the kind of behavior you expect from him. He will quickly pick on it. If you start following intuitive eating, your child will soon join you.

Challenge#5: Feeling different

At times, you might feel a little odd while raising an intuitive eater. You might get strange looks from your family members or others whenever they see your child eat. Or you might also start questioning your abilities as a parent. Well, you don't have to worry about all these things. Your child does eat differently from an average child, and that is fine. It is a good thing, and once you are aware of all the benefits your child can reap from intuitive eating, you will not worry about those looks anymore. Even today, society tends to focus more on what to feed children instead of how to feed them.

You might or might not run into all these challenges. All it takes is a little compassion, patience, and resilience to overcome these challenges. After all, it is not easy to teach new things to a child. So, be patient in the meantime. Once you start seeing an improvement in your child's relationship with food, you will realize that all your effort has been worth it.

Principles of Intuitive Eating

Intuitive eating is not just for adults, but it can be easily taught to kids as well. There are no rules when it comes to intuitive eating, but there are certain principles that have to be followed. These principles act as basic guidelines to ensure that you are on the right path. Once you start following these principles, you will see a positive change in the relationship you share with food. They are not difficult, and with a little conscious effort can be easily added to your daily life. The principles of intuitive eating are as follows.

Letting go of the diet mentality. You don't have to ever think about dieting again once you start eating intuitively. The human body is an efficient machine, and it knows what it needs. As long as you listen to its needs and requirements, and fulfill them, it will keep functioning optimally. So, follow this principle while dealing with your child. Have a little faith that his body knows what it needs.

Intuitive eating encourages you to make peace with food. It is about letting go of any labeling of food as either being good or bad. Once you stop labeling foods, your child will also start doing the same. Don't tell him that certain foods are good or bad. Allow him to decide for himself what he wants. By doing this, you are encouraging him to listen to his body.

You need to improve your relationship with food before you can start teaching the same to your child. So, it is time to challenge the food police. You don't have to feel guilty whenever you binge on any so-called bad foods. If you are worried about doing this, then maybe you can come up with healthier alternatives. For instance, potato chips can be replaced with baked kale chips.

Hunger is one of the most fundamental biological processes, and it is quite normal. Learning to honor and trust your body's cues is an essential part of intuitive eating. Try to encourage your child to tell you whenever he is hungry. Instead of sticking to a strict eating schedule, give him the flexibility to decide when he wants to eat. Don't force him to eat a meal merely because it is time for one.

Listen to your body and try to understand when you are hungry and when it is full. Mealtime needs to be about food, and nothing else. In fact, make it a family practice of having meals together.

It is a great way to catch up and unwind after a tiring day. While eating, keep all your gadgets away and concentrate only on the food you eat. By doing this, it becomes easier to understand when your tummy is full. Avoid allowing your child to eat while watching TV or spending time in front of a bright screen. It also shows him the importance of mindful eating.

Give yourself and your child a chance to understand what you both like and don't like to eat. Once you discover what your child wants to eat, you can start similarly making more foods using the same ingredients. It is easier to incorporate a variety of ingredients when you realize what he likes and dislikes. Also, once you stop labeling foods, his willingness to try different varieties will increase.

Never use food as an escape mechanism. Eating a pint of ice cream will not solve your problems, and a bag of cookies will not melt your worries away. Even if they make you feel better, this relief will be momentary. Once the sugar rush goes away, all the emotions that were left unaddressed will come running back. Instead, start processing and dealing with your feelings. Please encourage your child to share his feelings with you freely. Avoid using food as a parenting tool.

Start including some form of physical activity to your child's daily routine. It could be something as simple as running in the backyard for 20 minutes. As long as your child moves all the muscles in his body and does it daily, his physical health will improve. Not just your child, but even you should start practicing this simple principle. After a while, you will see a positive change in your overall health.

3

Myths About Intuitive Eating

When it comes to nutrition, intuitive eating includes the simple act of making peace with food and respecting the ability of your body to recognize cues of hunger, as well as fullness. It mostly helps reduce anxiety, body image issues, any obsession over food, guilt over obsessive eating, and promote body positivity. It enables you to foster a better relationship with food. Unlike fad diets, it is a different approach to health as well as wellness. By recognizing your body's natural cues, you become adept at understanding what your body needs and doesn't need. It is not a diet in the traditional sense. There are a couple of simple protocols you do need to follow when it comes to intuitive eating, but there are no hard and fast rules, unlike restrictive dieting.

Whenever something gains popularity, a lot of misconceptions about it start increasing. As a parent, it is your responsibility to take care of your child's health and nutrition. A young child is incapable of fending for himself, and you need to take care of all his needs. The habits your child develops will stay with him as he enters adulthood as well. So, if he has an unhealthy relationship with food, it will remain with him forever. Therefore, you need to be mindful of the habits you teach him. Before you start following the protocols of intuitive eating or learn to raise your child as an intuitive eater, there are certain myths you must be aware of.

In this section, let us look at some of the most popular myths about intuitive eating and the facts.

Myth #1: It is a Diet

One of the basic principles of intuitive eating is that it is not a diet. Before you can start practicing intuitive eating, you must get rid of the dieting mentality. There are no strict restrictions or rules you have to follow. You don't have to worry about the foods you can and cannot eat. Instead, intuitive eating primarily focuses on understanding your natural cues of hunger. Unlike a regular diet, it is more of an abstract idea than a rigid concept. Intuitive eating enables you to start looking at food from the perspective of hunger and satisfaction.

Myth #2: It has Rules

Most of the traditional diets like paleo, keto, Atkins, or any other detox diets, tend to have several rules and restrictions. Intuitive eating doesn't have any such restrictions. Instead, it encourages its followers to start developing a flexible structure. That being said, it does take a little control to learn to regulate one's eating habits. Learning to differentiate between genuine hunger and emotional eating also takes some practice. Intuitive eating is all about getting to understand one's body.

Myth #3: Eat Junk Food

Intuitive eating promotes the idea of eating like a child. A lot of people believe that "eating like a child," means eating junk food, sugary treats, and a whole range of unhealthy foods. Eating like a child does not indicate any of this. If you ever see children eat, you will realize that they eat with gusto, enthusiasm, curiosity, and absolute involvement. Apart from this, children also know when they are hungry and full. For instance, babies cry or start making the sucking motion with their mouth whenever they are hungry. Once their tummy is full, they probably sleep or stop crying. Intuitive eating is all about going back to one's roots to understand these things. As adults, most of us have become adept at ignoring our body's cues of hunger. In our rush to get things done, we forget to concentrate on ourselves.

Myth #4: No Physical Activity

Intuitive eating actually promotes the idea of physical activity. Add some form of physical exercise because it is quintessential for your overall well-being. Intuitive eating encourages you to come up with different activities that you enjoy. Most of the diets today tend to concentrate on weight loss or improving one aspect of your life. Intuitive eating encourages your overall development and growth. When you finally disassociate the concept of weight loss from exercising, your willingness to exercise will increase. When physical activity is not thrust upon you, you will start enjoying it.

Myth #5: It is Easy

The concept of intuitive eating is fairly simple. There are no precise instructions you have to follow. However, if you have been used to dieting, then shifting your mindset is a little tricky. Since there is no prize to win, learning to accept the principles of intuitive eating might not be quite straightforward. The right time to start with it is probably in childhood. Once a child gets used to eating intuitively, these habits will stick with him throughout his life. Well, even adults can start following the protocols of intuitive eating, provided they are willing to change their habits and mentality about food.

In spite of all these myths about intuitive eating, it is a brilliant approach towards improving one's health and nutrition. It helps establish a rather satisfying eating experience. Now that all these myths have been cleared up, your willingness to raise your child as an intuitive eater will increase.

4

Truth About Skipping Meals

Kids Must Not Skip Meals

The kind of meals, as well as snacks your child eats during the day, play a vital role in his physical as well as mental development. It is okay for your child to skip a meal occasionally, but making a habit of it is certainly not a good idea. Eating well-balanced, as well as nutritious meals, are essential for his overall development. Here are a couple of reasons why your child must not skip his meal regularly.

Energy and hunger

If your child doesn't eat timely meals, his energy levels will decrease. When he is low on energy, his irritability and crankiness increase. Apart from this, he will also feel extremely tired. The calories present in the meals are quintessential for providing him with energy for the day that lies ahead. It is not just breakfast, but he also needs to eat lunch, as well as dinner.

When he skips a meal, the protein, vitamins, minerals, and dietary fibers, he needs to concentrate and focus will reduce. Your child might also feel rather sluggish and might not be able to get much done. For instance, if he skips lunch, he might be exhausted to go about his day until he eats. When he runs low on energy, it can also induce headaches.

Educational delay

Your child's ability to concentrate and focus on his studies or education he receives at school will suffer if he doesn't get proper nutrition. Eating the right food at launch will give him the power he needs to concentrate on his studies. Brain fog is not just common in adults, but in children as well. Apart from this, eating unhealthy foods can cause fluctuations in his energy levels. For instance, he might feel quite energetic after eating a bowl of ice cream. However, once his body metabolizes all the sugar present in it, he will feel tired out. To avoid all this, he needs to eat well-balanced meals. A meal that consists of whole grains, vegetables, lean meat, healthy fats, and fruits will give his body the energy it requires to function optimally.

Lack of nutrition

What will happen if you don't water plants regularly? What will happen if you overwater them? Will the plants survive if they don't get sufficient sunlight? Well, the plants are bound to die in all these three cases. When the human body doesn't get adequate nutrition, it cannot function like it is supposed to.

Given that your child is still growing, his body needs plenty of nourishment. It is one of the main reasons why children need to snack frequently. Without well-balanced meals, your child might not get sufficient nutrients and vitamins his body needs.

Physical inactivity

He might not be motivated to engage in any after-school activities if he doesn't get proper meals. If you want your child to stay active, he needs nutritious meals. A well-balanced meal ensures that there are no fluctuations in his energy levels. When there are no sudden dips in his energy level, he will be more active. So, encourage your child not to skip any meals.

Urge to overeat

When your child skips a meal, his tendency to overeat will increase. It can also increase cravings for processed foods. A combination of these factors can lead to childhood obesity. Apart from this, it also encourages creating an unhealthy relationship with food. All these things go against the principles of intuitive eating.

One thing you must keep in mind is that you must never force your child to eat when he doesn't want to. There will be days when he wouldn't want to eat a meal or skip a snack, which is all right. As long as he doesn't get used to doing this regularly, don't force it. If you force him to eat even when he is full, it can lead to overeating and childhood obesity.

Stop Kids from Skipping Meals

It can be exceptionally frustrating when your child refuses to eat. Especially after you have spent a long time in the kitchen cooking something that you thought he would enjoy. There are different reasons why children tend to skip meals. Not just kids, but even teens tend to do this. In this section, let us explore some of the most common reasons why kids skip meals and what you can do about it.

Your child might refuse to eat whenever he feels like he's being pressured into eating. Keep in mind that mealtime must never be a source of anxiety for your child. If you start focusing on how much and when he eats, he will undoubtedly refuse to eat. Instead, encourage him to eat whenever he is hungry. Don't give him any directions or orders. You can certainly provide him with healthier alternatives, but don't come up with rules like,

"You cannot leave the table until you finish everything on your plate."

Also, don't set any specific times during which your child is supposed to eat. There will be instances when he feels hungry earlier than usual. Allow him to eat whenever he is hungry. It is the best way to ensure that he becomes an intuitive eater. Make mealtimes fun.

Your child might refuse to eat if he feels like he has no say. No one likes to feel helpless and out of control. It applies to your child too. Even if you think you know better than him, don't take his power away. If you start asking your child suggestions about what he would want to eat or how he would want you to cook certain things, he will feel like his opinions matter. Once he feels like his opinions matter and that he does have a say, he will be more inclined towards actively eating. Allow your child to choose what he wants to eat. Also, avoid feeding him the same food daily. If he starts getting bored with the food, he will not want to eat.

It is a good idea to give him a little control, but there needs to be certain boundaries as well. For instance, you cannot become a short-order cook and start cooking whatever your child wants whenever he wants. Instead, tell him about the different alternatives and encourage him to choose. It will take a while before he finally gets the hang of intuitive eating. In the meanwhile, you need to be extremely patient. The best way to get excited about mealtimes is to involve him whenever you are planning the menu, shopping for groceries, doing meal prep, or cooking.

Children refuse to eat whenever they are not hungry. Well, that should be obvious. If you're not hungry, you will not want to eat. Children tend to have a somewhat erratic eating schedule, and their appetite is often unpredictable. There will be days when your child will want to eat a lot and days when he refuses to eat anything at all. As long as you know your child is getting sufficient nourishment, whenever he eats is fine.

There will be certain foods your child loves. So, in your bid to try and get him to eat more, you might end up cooking the same varieties repeatedly. Well, if you do this, your child will certainly get bored with eating. There needs to be plenty of variety to choose from if you want him to become an intuitive eater. If he knows that his menu is going to be fixed for every single day of the week and that he will be eating the same meal daily, he will not want to eat at all. Encourage him to actively take part in all the meal planning that you too. Take into consideration his opinions about what he would want and not want to eat. While having this conversation, ensure that you keep an open mind and don't judge his preferences.

Keep in mind that your child's appetite will undoubtedly be smaller than your appetite. Not just that, even your child's ability to stomach food is quite limited. As they grow, their appetite increases and the portions he can consume will also increase. So, you cannot expect a five-year-old to eat the way a 13-year-old does. Maybe if you notice that there is food left on the plate every day, it is time to cut back on the portion size. Maybe start serving your child smaller portions. If your child wants more, he will ask for it. It is better than serving huge portions and then expecting him to finish it. Also, if your child ends up eating more than he needs, it will undoubtedly harm his overall well-being.

We all live in a world that's dominated by technology. Different gadgets continuously surround us. A lot of parents tend to give their children access to prolonged screen time because it keeps them thoroughly engaged and busy. However, if your child is watching TV, playing games, or doing something else, he will not be able to eat. If your child is distracted, then he will start skipping meals. Therefore, always make sure that mealtime is free from all distractions. It is a great way to teach your child about mindfulness as well. Why don't you start practicing the simple technique and encourage your child to do the same?

If the child is unwell, his appetite will reduce. It is often the first sign that he is feeling unwell. If that's the case, ensure that you give your child plenty of fluids and keep his body thoroughly hydrated. Apart from this, start giving him easily digestible foods. When your child is sick, he might not want to eat his favorite foods as well. It is okay. When his body is fully recovered, he will regain his appetite. You don't have to force-feed him. If you are worried, consult a pediatrician before you do anything.

Your child will certainly start skipping meals if he keeps getting too many snacks between mealtimes. It is impractical to expect a three-year-old to eat three huge meals when he gets to eat two snacks between every meal. It is a lot of food for his tiny body. Unless your child specifically asks for a snack after eating a filling meal, avoid giving him too many snacks. It is a great way to encourage him to become mindful of his hunger. Also, if you keep filling up your little one with plenty of fruit juices, his appetite for solid food will reduce.

If your child is too tired, then he will not want to eat. At times, kids might be so tired that even the thought of chewing and swallowing food doesn't appeal to them. There are instances when children just fall asleep while eating as well. Encourage your child to eat as much as he wants before bedtime. Also, start reminding him that he will not be able to eat anything

25

until breakfast the next morning. By doing this, you are setting certain boundaries about time restrictions. While following the guidelines of intuitive eating, you are free to eat whenever you want, but that doesn't mean you start eating dinner at 2 am.

5

Mindful Eating For Kids

I ntuitive eating, as well as mindful eating, might sound similar, but they are two different concepts altogether. Since they are both based on a non-diet approach towards health and nourishment, people tend to think of them as synonyms. They share certain similarities, but they are not the same. In this section, let us understand the differences between mindful eating and intuitive eating. Mindful eating is merely the application of mindfulness while eating.

Mindfulness is considered as a state of awareness that comes from consciously paying attention to the present moment without any judgment. Mindful eating enables you to become aware of the food you consume while encouraging you to think about how it will nourish your body, mind, and soul. Mindful eating helps you to start respecting and listening to your inner sense of wisdom while eating. It also means that you are supposed to eat your food with all your senses. Mindful eating encourages you to savor every morsel of food while relishing its textures, aroma, taste, and sight. While practicing the concept of mindful eating, you need to withhold any judgments. Regardless of whether you like something you or you don't like it, do not judge. It is about becoming physically aware of the cues of hunger as well as satiety.

Intuitive eating is about learning to make peace with all the foods you consume, becoming aware of your inner cues of hunger to derive satisfaction from the food you eat, and improving your overall health. Intuitive eating, as its name suggests, is an eating practice that is based on one's intuition. According to intuitive eating, it is believed that the human body knows what it needs. As long as people start paying attention to what their body requires, they can provide it with the kind of nourishment it needs.

There are plenty of similarities between intuitive eating and mindful eating. Both these approaches don't encourage the idea of dieting. Instead, they place greater emphasis on under-standing the internal cues of hunger. These practices don't encourage people to change the food they eat or reduce the quantity; instead they focus on how a person eats. It is not what you eat, but how you eat that matters. Neither of these methods encourages the classification of food. By restraining yourself from classifying and labeling certain foods as being good or bad, it helps strengthen the relationship you share with food. It is thought of as a natural technique that helps promote self-improvement along with your overall health.

The difference between these two concepts is that intuitive eating offers a broader framework, whereas mindful eating is just about being present in the moment while eating. It is about relishing the experience of eating without any judgment. Intuitive eating allows people to step outside and actively engage in eating while getting rid of a diet based mentality. A person can become a mindful eater without following the ideas of intuitive eating. However, an intuitive eater needs to be a mindful eater as well. Intuitive eating cannot exist without a little mindfulness. For instance, it is impossible to understand the internal cues of hunger and distinguish them from the external ones if you're not aware of yourself. Well, self-awareness does come from a degree of mindfulness.

So, intuitive eating can be easily combined with the philosophy of mindful eating. You can start encouraging your child to follow these techniques. Once he starts recognizing what hunger is and understands when his tummy is full, he can become more mindful of what he eats. When he stops judging himself for eating certain foods, he will feel better about himself. Apart from this, it will also give him a sense of confidence when he knows what he needs. The power to decide when he wants to eat, what he wants to eat, and how much he wants to eat will make him feel better about himself. When he knows that he is in charge of taking care of his health, his willingness to listen to you will also increase. Whenever your child is eating, encourage him to be present at the moment without thinking about anything else. So, if he wants to watch his favorite TV show while snacking, discourage him from doing this. Instead, tell him there is time for every activity in his schedule, and he doesn't need to combine anything.

Importance of Breakfast

Breakfast is believed to be the most important meal of the day. After all, as the name suggests, it is a great way to end the fast that your body is in a while you are asleep. So, if you want your child's body to stop fasting, then you need to give him some breakfast daily.

Consuming a healthy and well-balanced breakfast daily helps maintain your child's healthy weight. Since it can be anywhere between 8 to 10 hours before your child's last meal and breakfast, your child needs to break his fast. If his body is in a fasted state for too long, then it can lead to unnecessary weight gain.

It is essential that your child consumes a nutritious breakfast every morning to ensure that his body has sufficient energy for the day that lies ahead. It is a great way to ensure that he gets his daily dose of iron, fiber, vitamins, and folate.

Skipping breakfast can adversely affect your child's ability to concentrate. When his body doesn't have sufficient fuel it needs, or he ends up eating unhealthy foods, then he will feel tired. Not just this, it can also lead to unnecessary crankiness. It is a good idea to ensure that his breakfast contains foods with a low glycemic index and a high content of fiber and protein.

If your child is always in a rush to get to school or if your teen refuses to sit down and eat breakfast, you can always pack a snack for them. Something as simple as a tin of baked beans, yogurt, whole-grain cereal, a handful of nuts, and fruits or fruit juice can make for a good breakfast. However, don't encourage your child to eat on the go. Instead, try waking him up a little early so that he has time to sit down and eat a proper breakfast.

Kids tend to be fussy eaters. However, there are a couple of simple ways in which you can ensure that your child gets a delicious and nutritious breakfast. A bowl of whole-grain cereal with milk or even some yogurt along with sliced fruit is a great idea. Add in a couple of nuts, and it becomes more exciting to eat. You can serve him breakfast smoothie as well. Another simple idea is to serve a poached egg on a whole-wheat toast. Instead of eggs, you can use avocado as well.

Breakfast certainly is the most important meal of the day, so don't encourage your child to skip it. Also, you will need to start eating breakfast, if you are habituated to skipping it regularly. After all, your child will follow what he sees you, too. So, start setting a good example today.

6

Healthier Food Alternatives

K ids and adults alike enjoy junk food. How does the idea of healthy junk food sound? Does it sound too good to be true? Well, the good news is, it is possible. Even if it seems a little contradictory, you can always make junk food healthy. You don't have to compromise on taste for the sake of health. If you want to raise an intuitive eater, you need to offer him healthier alternatives to the foods he likes. Munching on chips might be your child's favorite snack, but it isn't good for him. Junk food is full of processed and unhealthy ingredients. It is primarily made up of empty calories. When a child starts feeding his body. All these undesirable foods, it tends to affect his overall growth. His body needs plenty of nutrition, and by feeding him junk food; you are only giving him access to oil, sugar, and salt along with unnecessary carbs. It can even lead to obesity while increasing his risk of several other health problems. If you want him to be healthy, then it is time to be mindful of the food he eats.

Telling your kids to stay away from junk food will not work. As an adult, even you might have difficulty stopping yourself from eating your favorite ice cream or drinking soda. So, if you cannot do it yourself, how can you expect a child to? Therefore, it is time to start coming up with healthier alternatives. If you start depriving your child of the food he likes, he will develop an unhealthy relationship with food.

In this section, let us look at some healthier alternatives for junk food.

Burgers

Who doesn't love a good burger? However, most burgers are full of trans fats and carbs. Who can resist the temptation of a delicious, juicy, and cheesy burger? Well, the good news is, there are healthy alternatives to this. Instead of deep-fried patties that are usually used, you can make these patties at home. The meat you choose matters. Instead of red meats, you can opt for lean poultry like turkey or skinless chicken. Top it with plenty of veggies and place it in between a whole-wheat bun! These days, there are plenty of gluten-free hamburger buns available as well that you can choose from. Or you can also use a tortilla wrap. Another alternative is to place the chosen fillings between a lettuce leaf.

You can make these burger patties in batches and freeze them for later. It certainly helps save plenty of time. If you want, you can prepare the mince and store it in freezer-safe boxes or pouches. Your child will undoubtedly love the healthier alternative because it not only looks like a burger but also tastes like one.

Pizza

A delicious slice of cheesy pizza is undoubtedly a hit with kids and adults alike. How about we make the regular pizza a little healthy? Instead of the regular pizza base made of processed flour, you can opt for cauliflower crust pizza. Apart from this, processed flour can be easily substituted with nut-based flours. It is quite easy to make pizza healthy. If you want, you can place all the pizza toppings on a tortilla. Allow your child to choose all the toppings he wants. When using cheese, try to opt for fresh mozzarella instead of the processed ones. Whenever possible, opt for fresh ingredients! They not only help elevate the flavors of food but are nutritious too.

French Fries

French fries are amongst the most popular fast food items. They are quite popular among children as well as adults. What is not to love about fries? Deep-fried potatoes sprinkled with salt make for a delicious treat. Chips make for not only a great snack, but also a side dish! French fries can be easily transformed into nutritious snacks. Instead of deep-frying potatoes in oil, you can fry them in an air fryer. In fact, most of the fried foods can be cooked in an air fryer by using just a couple of drops of oil. Alternatively, you can also roast them in the oven. Fries don't necessarily have to be restricted to potatoes. You can use sweet potatoes and any other hearty root vegetables of your choice. Carrots and zucchini can also be quickly turned into fries.

You no longer have to depend on fast food outlets or the frozen foods aisle to get delicious fries. You can start making them at home! Not only are they extremely nutritious, but they are also low in trans fats and other harmful fats. Your child can finally enjoy eating fries while you get the satisfaction of feeding him a healthy meal.

Potato Chips

Regardless of whether you call them chips or crisps, there is one thing we can all agree on- they are absolutely delicious. Potato chips are rather addictive. Forget one; it isn't possible to stop yourself once you start munching on chips. These days, potato chips are available in a variety of flavors. Your local supermarket will undoubtedly have a couple dozen varieties of colorful packs of different types of potato chips. Well, not only are these packets half full of air but they are also full of trans fat and salt. In fact, once you finish a bag of chips, you will be incredibly thirsty, and a cup of water might not quench your thirst.

Sadly, children seem to love and enjoy these chips. Chips are available in different flavors like salt and vinegar to barbecue, sour cream and onion, cheese, and pretty much any other flavor you can think of. You can easily outsmart these flaws by making them at home. You no longer have to deep fry them. Instead, start baking your chips. Instead of potato, you can also use plantain, kale, apples, and even sweet potatoes. The best part of doing this is that you are free to customize the flavors you want. Ask your child the flavors he would want to try and start adding them to the chips you make at home. Since you get to decide and control the ingredients you choose, you can opt for healthy cooking oil (olive oil or avocado oil) and make the chips less salty.

If your child is fussy about eating his greens, then add some kale chips to his usual meals. It is a great way to sneak in greens! You merely need to wash the kale leaves, season them with salt, sprinkle a little oil, along with any other seasonings you want and pop it in the oven. After a couple of minutes, you will have delicious and crispy kale chips. There is plenty of nutrition in every crunchy bite your child eats. They can easily be stored as well. You merely need a couple of airtight boxes or pouches to store these chips. Whenever your child feels hungry, you can grab them for him.

Candy

The sight of candy might remind you of Halloween or even your childhood. Parents often use candy as rewards as well as bribes to get their children to listen to them. Although these candies are full of nostalgia, they are rich in empty calories and sugars, along with preservatives. The only thing your child might get apart from momentary joy whenever he eats candy is a cavity. There are several healthy alternatives to sweets. One of the most straightforward options includes dehydrated fruit.

Making dehydrated fruit at home is quite easy. In fact, these days, there is dehydrated fruit available in the market as well. However, while buying any food product, ensure that you carefully read the labels on the packet. Go through the nutritional information along with the list of ingredients. If there are any ingredients that you don't recognize or sound too complicated, then it's a good idea to stay away from it.

All that you need to do is thinly slice your favorite fruit, place them on a parchment or silicone baking sheet, and then bake them in the oven. Yes, it is as simple as that. Within an hour or two, you will have dehydrated fruit ready. They are naturally sweet, contain no added sugars, and are a great way to get your kids to eat fruit!

Pasta or Noodles

A bowl of noodles or pasta certainly makes for a comforting meal. Children seldom say no to spaghetti and meatballs! Not only are these dishes quite easy to cook, but whenever you are in a rush, instant noodles certainly make things easier. With the increasing popularity of instant noodles, there are several flavors available in the market these days. They are delicious, but they don't contain any nutritional value whatsoever. The same stands for prepackaged pasta like spaghettiOs. Prepackaged and canned kinds of pasta are certainly not healthy. Even if they save plenty of time in the kitchen, they are full of empty calories. These options are quite popular, but they are made from 100% processed ingredients and added flavors. So, there's nothing natural about them in the end.

Instead of relying on these things, you can start making pasta and noodles at home. It is a great idea to purchase a spiralizer and turn simple vegetables like carrots, zucchini, and cucumbers into noodles and pasta. So, if your child loves spaghetti Bolognese, all that you need to do is serve the Bolognese sauce or the meatballs and sauce on a bed of spiralized zucchini and carrots. Zucchini noodles or zoodles can also be used to make stir-fries. Cooking this kind of healthier noodles is quite easy.

If you like the idea of batch cooking, then you can make the spaghetti or noodle sauce while in advance and freeze them for later. So, whenever your child is hungry, all that's left for you to do this quickly toss some healthy noodles or pasta and heat up the sauce.

Breakfast Cereal

Breakfast cereal is a big hit with kids. From Lucky charms to Cocoa puffs, oat flakes, and several other varieties, there are plenty of options to choose from. It is perhaps one of the reasons fast food and junk food are quite tempting. All the varieties available these days can tempt anyone. Breakfast cereals, along with energy drinks were considered to be among healthy options available in the market or as a health food. However, the reality is quite different. Breakfast cereal contains plenty of carbs and hidden sugars. Apart from this, the ingredients used in the cereals are processed to the extent that they don't retain any of their primary nutritional value. Therefore, convenience certainly comes at a considerable cost. If you want your child to start off his day with a healthy breakfast, then don't opt for prepackaged breakfast cereal.

So, what can be done? Well, even breakfast cereal can be made healthy. You can make granola at home. Purchase some good quality rolled oats, puffed quinoa, or any other superfoods you can think of and combined them with your choice of nuts and dried fruits. Add a dash of dark cocoa powder to this mix and voila! Breakfast cereal is now ready! You can fashion them into bite-sized chewy bars too.

Cookies

Chocolate chip cookies are perhaps amongst the most loved flavor of cookies. They're crunchy on the outside, chewy on the inside, and thoroughly chocolaty. Perhaps this is the best way to describe chocolate chip cookies. A freshly baked cookie, along with a cold glass of milk, might remind you of your childhood. Biting into a delicious cookie is a rather pleasant feeling. However, this happiness also comes at a price. All chocolate chip cookies available in the market these days contain high amounts of added sugars, trans fats, and carbs. All the things that your child is not required to eat are present in large quantities. The refined flour and chemical preservatives just make things worse.

Instead of store-bought cookies, you can find healthier alternatives like making whole-wheat chocolate chip cookies. These cookies can be made easily by using whole wheat flour, chocolate chips, and bananas. Yes, that's about it. You just need three ingredients to make delicious cookies. If your child has any dietary restrictions, then try the gluten-free and dairy-free variants.

Ice Cream

There are very few things that can match the joy of digging into a frozen treat. There is nothing better than a cup of your favorite ice cream on a sunny day. Well, your child must be feeling the same. Ice cream is undoubtedly delicious, but it mainly consists of unnecessary sugars, milk solids, and artificial flavors that mimic natural fruits. Well, that certainly is a killjoy.

Instead of ice cream, you can give your child frozen yogurt. Yogurt not only helps improve the health of your child's gut bacteria but is low in carbs and calories as well. So, by giving your child a scoop of frozen yogurt, you are effectively improving his health. Encourage him to top up the yogurt with his favorite toppings like dried fruits or even the breakfast cereal you've made at home. Making frozen yogurt is quite simple. You merely need to blend yogurt along with all the other ingredients and flavorings you want to add, and then transfer it into an airtight container and freeze it. Once it hardens, frozen yogurt is ready. Frozen yogurt can be made in a variety of flavors ranging from chocolaty to fruity ones.

If not frozen yogurt, then you can always opt for nice creams. Nice creams are ice creams made using frozen bananas! Banana nice creams are vegan. They are known as nice creams because they mimic the classic texture of ice cream but don't contain any of the unhealthy calories and sugars. So, all that you need to do is blend some frozen bananas, along with a little almond milk, and any other additional flavorings you want, such as chocolate chips, cocoa powder, or even dried fruit. Once the mixture resembles a purée, it needs to be placed in the freezer. After an hour or two, it can be easily scooped up like regular ice cream.

These two options are quite easy to make and don't require any fancy ingredients. Children will certainly love them because they pretty much look like ice cream and taste like ice cream! So, what's not to love?

Soda and Fruit Juices

Whenever your child drinks fruit juice, you might be quite happy that he is consuming fruit in some form. However, never opt for the packaged fruit juices. Just like any other form of junk food, even pre-packaged fruit juices contain plenty of sugars and unhealthy artificial flavorings. If you are really interested in making your little one eat fruits, it is always better to make fruit juices at home. All that you need to do is merely toss in the required fruits into a juicer and wait for the appliance to work its magic. Also, whenever possible, try to get your child to eat whole fruits instead of fruit juices. All the dietary fiber present in the fruit is often lost when they are turned into juices.

Saying no to soda is not that easy. Regardless of whether it is regular diet sodas, they contain chemicals as well as dyes along with unhealthy sugars, which are certainly not good for your child's body. Not just for your child, but sodas are not good for anyone. Sodas can be easily replaced with sparkling water! Take some sparkling water, muddle it with some fresh fruit and mix them together. If not, natural fruit juice can also be added to sparkling water. So, whenever your child craves for some fizzy beverage, you can give him this instead of regular soda. Also, the sugar content in sodas is quite high. If you don't want your child to be bouncing off the walls after drinking soda, then opt for fruit juices. Soda can also be replaced with lemonade and homemade iced tea.

Cupcakes

Your child might have the biggest smile on his face when he knows that he can eat a cupcake. Everyone loves cupcakes. No wonder they have become quite popular and a permanent fixture at all children's parties, as well as celebrations. These days, cupcakes are available in beautiful designs, creating a culture of designer cupcakes as well. Cupcakes are often made of refined flours and sugars, not to mention the sugary frosting. They will certainly make a child happy, but as you know, they have no nutritional value whatsoever.

So, what if you could make cupcakes that look and taste like cupcakes, but are quite healthy? Instead of using refined flour, you can opt for whole-wheat flour, almond flour, flour made of any other whole grains, or any other nut-based flours. By simply replacing a couple of ingredients with healthier alternatives, you can ensure that your child gets a steady dose of nutrition without compromising on taste. So, the next time your child starts eating cupcakes that you bake at home, you have nothing to worry about. Another great thing is like any other junk food recipe, these cupcakes can also be baked in batches and stored for later. Ensure that you don't store them for longer than a week.

Chocolates

Does your kid love chocolates? Does he get cranky whenever you deny him chocolates? Whenever you both go to your local supermarket, does he demand that you purchase chocolate for him? Chocoholics come in various shapes, sizes, and age groups. Now, if only you could somehow magically turn this unhealthy bar of chocolate into something delicious and healthy. Well, you are in for a treat!

Chocolate bark is not only easy to make, but you can also make it using pretty much any of the ingredients you have in your pantry. So, you don't need to splurge on any expense ingredients. Apart from this, you can make them in batches and even used as a party snack. You need to melt some good quality dark chocolate chips, preferably the ones that don't contain any added sugar. Add finely chopped nuts, dried fruit, or even healthy muesli to this mixture. Spread this mixture thinly on a sheet of parchment, and once it solidifies, you can cut it into smaller chunks.

Another great idea is to dip nuts and dried fruits into melted chocolate and freeze them for later. Also, you can use this technique to make chocolate-coated strawberries too! Think of all the different ingredients you can combine with chocolate and get started. If you do want to add any sugar to it, use only natural sweeteners like Stevia and stay away from processed sugars.

Mac and Cheese

Mac and cheese is often deemed as comfort food for a lot of people. Yes, the creamy and cheesy sauce is certainly quite comforting and will lift your spirits up, especially when you're low, but it is extremely unhealthy as well. There are plenty of ready to eat mac and cheese variations available in the market these days. The yellow cheese sauce is a sad excuse for the natural goodness of milk and healthy cheeses. This, combined with preservatives, added flavorings, and undesirable carbs, certainly makes the ready-to-eat variants unhealthy.

The good news is that you can start making mac and cheese

at home. It hardly takes 20 minutes to whip up a delicious and healthy batch of mac and cheese. You can easily replace all the unhealthy saturated fats and calories with low-cal and delicious variants. These days, there are different types of pasta available in the market as well. Choose whole-grain pasta and not the highly processed variants available. If you want, you can make pasta at home as well. If you have a pasta maker, it certainly makes your life easier. Also, instead of the traditional cheese sauce, you can make a gluten-free variant using pureed cauliflower. So, your child gets to eat mac and cheese without clearly consuming all the unhealthy fats and calories. Also, try adding in a couple of other toppings to the mac and cheese you make at home. Ranging from grilled chicken to sautéed vegetables, add whatever toppings your child asks for (as long as they are healthy).

Milkshake

Turn your child away from milkshakes and towards the warm embrace of homemade smoothies. Whenever it is hot outside and your child is craving something sweet to drink, fruit juices are available. However, he will certainly get bored of fruit juices, after a while. Therefore, try adding a couple of different homemade smoothies to the mix. Making smoothies is quite simple. In fact, a smoothie can be an entire meal by itself.

A smoothie is a blended juice that contains fruits, vegetables, and dairy products, such as yogurt or milk. Smoothies can be a mix of pretty much anything that you want. Also, you can start sneaking in vegetables as well as fruits into your child's daily diet by giving him smoothies. Smoothies are not only easy to make, but you can even give him a smoothie for breakfast. It is not just a snack, but a meal by itself. All that you need to do is toss and all the ingredients into a blender and just blended for a minute or two. Once ready, serve it immediately. You can even add breakfast cereal like hand-rolled oats, muesli, or even cornflakes to the smoothies you make.

Chocolate Spread

It is hard to find someone who can resist the urge of licking clean a spoon of delicious and gooey chocolate spread like Nutella. There are several other delicious variants of chocolate spreads available in the market these days. They are certainly delicious but have extremely high-calorie count as well. One hundred grams of Nutella contains about 550 calories! Phew, that's a lot of calories for maybe six tablespoons of Nutella! Neither you nor your child can afford to scarf down calories at this rate.

Well, you can make chocolate spread at home! Also, the chocolate spreads you make at home are not only delicious and healthy but are light on your pocket as well. To make healthy chocolate spread at home, you need to combine hazelnuts with unsweetened cocoa powder, and full-fat milk of your choosing, maple syrup, unrefined salt, and some vanilla extract. The number of ingredients you use will depend on the consistency you are looking for. Once ready, transfer it into some fancy glass jars and store it for later.

Peanut Butter

One hundred grams of peanut butter contains close to 600 calories! Peanut butter and jelly sandwiches are something everyone loves. So, it is a combination of three absolutely unhealthy foods. Well, it can be quickly turned into a healthy sandwich! Instead of white bread, opt for whole-grain bread like rye or multigrain bread. Instead of purchasing peanut butter, you can start making peanut butter at home. You merely need to blitz peanuts and a little salt until it reaches the desired consistency. It can be additionally sweetened with a little honey. Homemade peanut butter is a healthier alternative to the store-bought variants. Your child will never be able to tell the difference between the healthy and unhealthy versions of peanut butter.

Brownies

A rich and gooey chocolate brownie can make anyone go weak in their knees. There's just something sinfully decadent about a rich chocolate brownie. Perhaps it is the slightly crunchy exterior, coupled with the wonderfully gooey center that makes people crave for them. Well, it is no wonder that children love brownies. If you have ever baked a batch of brownies, then you must be aware of all the butter and sugar that goes in. Instead of processed wheat flour, you can use whole wheat flour, sweeten the brownies using honey, and instead of butter, you can opt for some fresh yogurt. There are different, healthier alternatives available. If you want, you can also add in the peanut butter or chocolate spread using the suggestions mentioned above. They can also be used as toppings for brownies.

Donuts

There are several international donut chains these days, and they all serve a variety of delicious donuts. There's just some-thing extremely tempting about freshly fried dough served with a liberal topping of sugar that seems to make children and adults go crazy for them. They are packed with more sugar than you can probably imagine and are rich in trans fats. However, they don't necessarily have to be unhealthy. Instead of deep-frying them, you can also bake them.

To make delicious donuts at home, you merely need to swap all the unhealthy ingredients with their healthier variations. For instance, instead of regular oil, you can opt for olive oil; instead of eggs, you can use banana, and processed flour can be replaced with almond flour. Don't allow your imagination to curtail you from coming up with healthier alternatives for the foods your kid loves. The great news is that the healthier alternatives taste pretty much like their original versions. So, your child can dig into all the treats he wants to, and you don't have to worry about his overall nutritional intake.

Cream-filled cookies

Perhaps the first thing you can think about whenever you think of cream-filled cookies is Oreos. The thought of separating the two cookies, licking of the delicious white cream present between them, and then dunking them in milk does sound wonderful. Even your child might enjoy doing this. Oreos are amongst the most popular cream-filled cookies out there. They are certainly delicious but are full of refined ingredients. Well, you can start making these cream-filled cookies at home.

Start by whipping up a batch of healthy and nutritious cookies. Once the cookies are ready, you merely need to make the cream filling. To make the cream filling, you can opt for coconut cream instead of the sugary icing. The coconut cream can be sweetened with a natural sweetener like stevia or honey. In fact, you can also fill it with some nice cream or healthy ice cream.

Chicken Nuggets

Crispy fried chicken nuggets served with some ketchup will certainly make a kid happy. There are over 300 calories present in 100 grams of McDonald's chicken nuggets. That's quite a high-calorie count, especially when you take into consideration that it is a mixture of leftover pieces of chicken and breadcrumbs. Instead of these unhealthy chicken nuggets, you can make healthier ones at home. Whenever possible, try to bake and don't opt for deep frying. If you want, you can always invest in an air fryer. An air fryer can be used for frying a variety of foods, and it hardly needs any oil. By dipping the pieces of chicken into the whisked egg and rolling it in panko crumbs, you can ensure that you aren't feeding an unhealthy batter to your little one. Then all that's left for you to do is simply bake it instead of deep-frying. You can use the same trick whenever you are making chicken wings as well. These foods look and taste just as delicious as their unhealthy counterparts!

Pretzels

Regardless of whether the pretzels are crunchy or soft, all kids love them. Giving your child pretzels might seem like an easy snack idea. However, they are full of processed carbs, trans fats, and plenty of salt. Instead of pretzels, you can give him popcorn! Once again, make this popcorn at home instead of buying the readymade varieties available in the market these days. All that you need are some dried corn kernels. Place them in a popcorn kettle along with any seasonings you want and voila! Fresh and delicious popcorn is ready within no time. You can also add any of your favorite toppings.

Popsicles

The thought of cold and refreshing Popsicle on a hot sunny day is amazing. Popsicles are merely made of food coloring, extra sugar, preservatives, and added flavorings. There is nothing healthy about popsicles. If you don't want to deprive your little one of this delicious snack, then there are healthier alternatives available. Did you know that an eleven-year-old accidentally invented the Popsicle?

Choose a Popsicle mold of your choice, fill it up with fruit juice, and freeze it! Now, your child can enjoy popsicles while getting his daily dose of fruits as well. Apart from fruit juices, you can even freeze smoothies using the Popsicle molds.

Pre-Packaged Dips

Buying a jar of mayonnaise, cheese dips, salsa, or any other pre-packaged dips certainly saves a lot of time and effort. These prepackaged foods are incredibly unhealthy. They are full of different additives and preservatives. Eating healthy includes eating natural foods. Instead of providing your child with foods that have been mass-produced in a factory, it is better to feed him home-cooked meals. It hardly takes any time to make these tips at home. Perhaps the quickest dip you can make is salsa. You merely need to chop some tomatoes, onions, and cilantro finely, and add some salt and lemon juice. It is as simple as that! Making cheese dips and mayonnaise at home is equally easy. Serve it with a side of whole wheat crackers, baked tortilla chips, or even pita bread. Apart from this, you can also make hummus at home. The alternatives available are unlimited.

When you start cooking everything at home, it gives you complete control over the ingredients you use. By opting for good-quality ingredients and using healthy oils for cooking, you are increasing your child's intake of nutritional foods. If the food tastes the same, your child will not complain. Also, in the long run, cooking at home is more pocket-friendly than eating out.

Apart from this, there are several other healthier alternatives for every food item these days. All it takes is a little creativity and imagination. Start using the different alternatives discussed in this section, and experiment in the kitchen. In fact, a simple Google search will give you hundreds of ideas. As long as you are willing to cook, you can provide your child with healthy and nutritious foods. Even you can start eating healthier. If you want, you can start getting your child involved whenever you are planning meals. Ask him what he would like to eat. By doing this, he will also feel like he has some say over what he eats. While cooking, he can be a little help in the kitchen.

Get Your Child to Eat Better

It is excellent that you are willing to try out different, healthier alternatives to junk food your child might usually be attracted to. However, it might not be of much help unless your child is willing to eat better. So, what can you do if your child is hooked onto unhealthy food? Well, there are specific simple tips you can start following to encourage your child to develop healthy eating habits.

Instead of focusing on specific foods that you think he must eat, concentrate on his overall diet. Try minimizing the number of processed foods he consumes while increasing the portions of wholesome foods.

If your child is a fussy or picky eater, then it is time to start disguising the taste of healthier foods. You can certainly use different recipes discussed in the previous section to hide the taste of healthy foods and disguise them to resemble the foods your kid loves. However, there is another simple trick you can start using as well. Whenever you're making any curries or sauces, and stews, start adding vegetables to them. Whenever you give your child some form of dessert, try adding more fruits to it. If you are willing to experiment a little, there are endless options about how you can make your child eat healthier foods.

Children love to imitate adults. It is how they start learning about life. So, be mindful of the food choices you make, and your attitude towards eating. If you display a positive attitude and are open to trying new foods, then your child will also follow suit. However, if your child sees other adults picking at their vegetables or refusing to eat certain foods, then he will even start doing the same. Therefore, be mindful of the way you conduct yourself around your child.

Children often need a couple of snacks between their meals. Not just children, but even adults, need snacks to ensure that their energy levels stay stable. Make sure that there are plenty of healthy snacks available to your little one. So, if he does fill his tummy up with these healthy treats, you don't have to worry too much.

Start cooking as many meals at home instead of eating out

every day, ordering takeout, or depending on convenience foods. A simple suggestion to get your child more interested in sampling various foods is by encouraging him to help you whenever you cook or do any meal prep. You can start cooking in batches and freeze certain items like sauces, stews, curries, soups, broths, and so on. So, whenever you need to eat, all that's left to do is merely reheat the frozen foods. Also, cooking at home is certainly more cost-effective and nutritious than eating out.

7

Get Started With Intuitive Eating For Kids

As a parent, you might be worried that your little one is not getting all the nutrition he requires because of his eating habits. It certainly is easier to talk to an adult than force an irritable child. If your child is a picky eater, then dealing with his strange eating habits can be a little tricky. If he doesn't finish his veggies, you might withhold dessert. Perhaps you decide to bargain with him that if he eats all of his food without any fuss, he can play for longer. Most parents tend to do these things, but it goes against the principles of intuitive eating.

By resorting to such techniques, unknowingly, you end up damaging his relationship with food in the long run. Instead of doing all this, teach him about intuitive eating. Intuitive eating is not a complicated topic, but teaching it to a child might not necessarily be easy. However, after going through all the information discussed in this book, you will realize all the benefits of intuitive eating. It can help bolster your child's relationship with food, as well as his body image. If you want to raise a child as an intuitive eater, then here are a couple of simple steps you can start using today.

Being Present

Mealtime needs to be a family activity. Even if you lead a hectic life, always make time to have at least one meal together. Whenever you are eating together, avoid checking your phone, or any other gadgets. Be present and make mealtime a priority. If you want your child to develop healthy habits, then you need to model the same.

No Negotiation with Food

Negotiating is a great way to defuse an argument. It might enable you to see what the other person wants. However, the dinner table is not a place for any negotiation whatsoever. Even if your child starts pouting or throws a tantrum, never bargain with him. If he thinks that he can get his way by resorting to this, then he will keep at it. Remember, you are an adult, and you have all the power. If your child sees food as a chore or even a burden, then his relationship with food, in the long run, will be damaged. Instead, encourage him to look at it as a source of nutrition as well as fun.

Flexibility

Having a routine is good since it gives your child a sense of security because of the predictability it offers. When your child knows he needs to eat three meals a day, along with two snacks, he will know what to expect. However, there needs to be a little flexibility too. There will be days when your child is not hungry, and he might not want to eat a meal or two. As long as you know he is not starving himself, allow him a little flexibility. Encourage your child to respond to what his body is telling him. It will certainly help him become an intuitive eater.

Accept When They are Full

You might have cooked a delicious meal, and your child might eat three bites before declaring that he is full. When this happens, resist the urge to say, "You are not done. Eat your food" or, "You aren't getting up from the table until your plate is clean." It is incredibly difficult for a parent, but try it once and see for yourself. At most, you can ask him whether he would want to eat a little more before getting up from the table. You might not want to believe it, but children certainly know when they are full. Usually, they tend to get all the nutrition the body needs from different meals and snacks they consume. As long as you keep feeding him healthy and nutritious meals and snacks, you have nothing to worry about. When you start respecting the things he says, he will be more inclined to listen to you as well.

Power of Food

Avoid labeling food as being good or bad. Not just that, but also refrain yourself from labeling yourself or anyone who eats certain types of foods as being good or bad. Instead, think of how healthy foods will help your little one. Even if your child rejects a couple of options you present him with, keep trying. Offer a variety of foods, and eventually, he will end up discovering vegetables and fruits he loves. When he enjoys eating healthy foods, you don't have to force him.

Provide them Options

Don't get too obsessed with getting your child to eat healthy foods. If you start forcing him to eat certain foods just because you know they are good for him, he might resist. Instead, begin offering a variety of foods. In fact, use the different healthy alternatives for junk food discussed in the previous chapters. Eating junk food isn't bad, especially when it is made with wholesome ingredients. So, start experimenting in the kitchen, come up with healthier alternatives, and offer them to your child. Your child will be more inclined to oblige your request when he starts enjoying the food he eats. Also, there needs to be some variety, and if the food starts getting monotonous, he will lose interest. It is not just true for children, but even adults as well. If you had to eat the same meal every single day of the week, even you would get bored.

Reward for Eating

If you reward your child for eating, it certainly sends the wrong message. After all, he is supposed to eat healthy and nutritious meals for his overall well-being. It is non-negotiable. If your child starts eating because he knows he will be rewarded when he cleans his plate, he will not grasp the importance of nutrition. Don't use screen time, extra playtime, dessert, or anything else as a form of reward. It can be quite tempting to praise him whenever he eats veggies. However, if you keep doing this, he will never learn to enjoy his mealtime.

Emotional Eating

Most of us tend to eat as a response to certain emotions we feel like fear, anxiety, boredom, or even sadness. We all do this, and it is time to recognize this habit. Resist the temptation of bingeing on any unhealthy, sugary, or carb-laden treats whenever your emotions are running high. If your child starts throwing a tantrum or is visibly upset because of something, don't offer a cookie or any other food item he likes. It might calm him down, but it doesn't help address his emotions. Also, unknowingly you are getting him habituated to emotional eating. Emotional eating is not suitable for anyone. Learn to process your feelings and encourage your child to do the same.

Your Behavior

Children tend to learn a lot from the way their parents and other adults behave around them. You might not realize it, but your child pays a lot of attention to the way you behave. If you are following a crash diet, and you feel the urge to hide it from your child, ask yourself why. Would you want your child to make the same food choices that you are making? If your answer is no, then it might not be the right choice for you as well. Instead, start following the principles of intuitive eating yourself. Always lead by example, when it comes to parenting.

Food as a Reward

It might sound quite similar to the previous one, but it is slightly different. Never use food as a form of reward. If your child does well in school, wins the match, or anything else, avoid rewarding him with food. There are different ways in which you can reward your child, and food isn't one of them. Avoid saying, "Let's go get you ice cream for cleaning your room," or, "Why don't we eat French fries because you did well at school?"

Well, what do you do when he doesn't clean his room, get good grades, or lose a match? When you start using fried foods or other junk food as a positive reward, you end up sending a mixed message to your child. He might start believing that certain foods are off-limits until he does something specific. He might also believe that food is a reward for good behavior. Both of these messages will not do him any good.

8

Conclusion

A significant concern a lot of parents have these days is whether their children get all the nourishment and nutrition their bodies require from their meals. If you are worried about your child's nutritional requirements, then it is time you start encouraging him to become an intuitive eater. Intuitive eating is a straightforward idea of eating that helps you to rely on your body's internal cues of hunger. Instead of allowing external signals to regulate appetite, you start paying attention to your body's needs. As the name suggests, it is about depending on your intuition when it comes to eating. Understanding the meaning of real hunger and cues of fullness and satisfaction are all part of intuitive eating.

The concept of intuitive eating is not just applicable to adults but to kids as well. The sooner you start, the better it is. Once your child gets the hang of intuitive eating, these practices will become a permanent habit. Intuitive eating will help children understand when they are hungry, not use food as a coping mechanism, and make a conscious decision to eat until they are full. Once children start following all this, there will be a change in their overall health as well.

In this book, there were plenty of healthy alternative options given for popular junk food. Now that we have reached the end of the book, you must have realized how easy it is to get your child to eat healthier. All that you need is a little creativity. There are plenty of healthy recipes and alternatives available online. Spend a little time and do your research. Also, always lead by example when it comes to parenting. If you expect your child to follow the guidelines of intuitive eating, then you need to follow your own advice! Learn to deal with all the frustrations and challenges that parenthood throws your way. In the meanwhile, don't forget to enjoy time with your little one. Intuitive eating is a great way to encourage him to develop a healthy relationship with food.

Resources

- 10 Ways to Get Started with Intuitive Eating for Kids | Think or Blue. Retrieved from https://www.thinkorblue. com/intuitive-eating-for-kids/
- Burns, J. https://www.parents.com. Retrieved from https: //www.parents.com/kids/nutrition/healthy-eating/get-your-kids-to-eat-better/
- Five Myths of Intuitive Eating | Lifespan. Retrieved from https://www.lifespan.org/lifespan-living/five-myths-intuitive-eating
- Kuzemchak, S. (2019). https://www.parents.com. Retrieved from https://www.parents.com/recipes/scoop-on-food/how-to-raise-intuitive-eaters-and-why-thats-so-important/
- Linn. (2016). Mindful Eating vs Intuitive Eating - Straightforward Nutrition. Retrieved from http:// www.straightforwardnutrition.com/mindful-eating-vs-intuitive-eating/
- Remmer, S. (2019). 10 Reasons Why Your Child Isn't Eating at Meals (and What to Do!). Retrieved from https://www.sarahremmer.com/10-reasons-why-your-child-isnt-eating-at-meals-and-what-to-do/
- Rumsey, A. (2019). What Is Intuitive Eating and How Is It Different From Mindful Eating?. Retrieved from https:

//alissarumsey.com/intuitive-eating/what-is-intuitive-eating/

· Underwood, R., May, M., & Camden, E. (2015). 5 Obstacles That Keep Parents from Raising Intuitive Eaters. Retrieved from https://maryannjacobsen.com/5-obstacles-that-keep-parents-from-raising-intuitive-eaters/